GOD'S CANVAS

Written by
Elizabeth Alfheim

Edited by
Julia Grant

Quail Acres Publishing
Imagination is Priceless!

ISBN: 979-8-9905163-3-5 Paperback

Quail Acres Publishing
www.elizabethalfheim.com

Printed and bound in the United States of America

About the Author

Elizabeth Alfheim, a beloved
teacher and now a bestselling
children's book author,
weaves captivating stories
that spark fantastical
journeys and draw little readers
into the enchanting world of storytelling.
Her trilogy, The Adventures of Beckham Grey, and
her alliteration series that includes Piddle Puddle Poodle
and Dilly-Dally Duck are current examples of her commitment to
making reading fun and learning impactful. Her dedication to literacy is
reflected in her acclaimed career as an educator, earning her the prestigious
"Educator of the Year" award. Elizabeth's love for God and His Word coupled
with her appreciation of His vibrant colors displayed on Earth have inspired
this story. If you're looking to ignite a child's passion for reading or nurture
their creative spirit, then find a comfortable seat and gather your little ones
around you, and let God's color display and words speak to your heart.

Do you ever stop to look and see
God's paintings done masterfully?

"*Praise the LORD, all his works everywhere in his dominion. Praise the LORD, my soul.*"
Psalm 103:22 NIV

His palette fills the land, sea, and sky
adorned with hues of endless supply.

"The sea is his, for he made it,
and his hands formed the dry land."
Psalm 95:5 NIV

With elegant strokes splashed here and there
and brilliant colors oh so fair,

no two paintings can ever be
an exact colorful jubilee.

"The earth takes shape like
clay under a seal;
its features stand out
like those of a garment."
Job 38:14 NIV

The distant peaks of mountain tops
and slopes as a valley drops

draw you into a landscape so vast
whispering tales of centuries past.

"Your righteousness is like the highest mountains,
your justice like the great deep ..."
Psalm 36:6 NIV

God's hand put each
mountain in place
adding trees and plants
the hillside to grace.

"Before the mountains were born
or you brought forth the whole world,
from everlasting to everlasting you are God."
Psalm 90:2 NIV

The various colors are
beyond what mere man could do.
Only the Great I Am
could create so majestic a view.

*"You are worthy, our Lord and God,
to receive glory and honor and power,
for you created all things, and by your will
they were created and have their being."*
Revelation 4:11 NIV

Look closely at each tree, plant, and flower. Be amazed at God's creative power.

"The land produced vegetation:
plants bearing seed according
to their kinds and trees bearing fruit
with seed in it according to their kinds.
And God saw that it was good."
Genesis 1:12 NIV

Focus in as vibrant blooms dot the space
a myriad of colors each set in place.

Gaze upon it all, a feast for the eye.
A paint stroke only the Creator could apply.

"For, 'All people are like grass,
and all their glory is like the flowers of the field;
the grass withers and the flowers fall,
but the word of the Lord endures forever.'
And this is the word that was preached to you."
1 Peter 1:24-25 NIV

The sky in its vastness whether day or night
the stars, moon, or sun's radiant, pure light

set the background with elegance and flair
a gorgeous picture that none can compare.

"The whole earth is filled with awe at your wonders;
where morning dawns, where evening fades,
you call forth songs of joy."
Psalm 65:8 NIV

Everywhere you look,
God's artwork is on display,
beauty beyond understanding
in a vivid array.

"The heavens declare the glory of God;
the skies proclaim the work of his hands."
Psalm 19:1 NIV

The birds of the air
and fish of the sea
animals abound,
a picturesque scene.

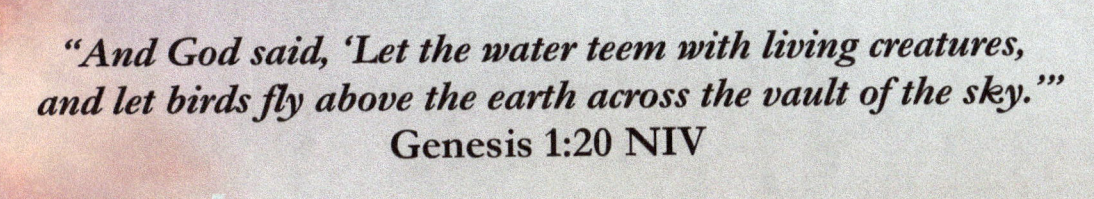

"*And God said, 'Let the water teem with living creatures,*
and let birds fly above the earth across the vault of the sky.'"
Genesis 1:20 NIV

Creatures on land
that scurry and race,
God put each species
right into place.

All things were created when time began
always a part of His grand plan.

The Alpha and Omega with paintbrush in hand
formed Adam in HIS image, the first man.

*"So God created mankind in his own image,
in the image of God he created them;
male and female he created them."*
Genesis 1:27 NIV

*"For we are God's handiwork,
created in Christ Jesus to do good works,
which God prepared in advance for us to do."*
Ephesians 2:10 NIV

The canvas once blank,
burst forth at His voice
singing a hallelujah,
a heavenly rejoice.

We are HIS masterpiece;
HIS art fills the land.
God said it was good,
all fulfilled by HIS hand.

"For this is what the Lord says--
he who created the heavens, he is God;
he who fashioned and made the earth, he founded it;
he did not create it to be empty, but formed it to be inhabited--
he says: 'I am the Lord, and there is no other.'"
Isaiah 45:18 NIV

Seven Days of Creation

Click on the QR Codes for a Creation Lesson!

"And God said, 'Let there be light,' and there was light. God saw that the light was good, and he separated the light from the darkness. God called the light 'day,' and the darkness he called 'night.' And there was evening, and there was morning—the first day."
Genesis 1:3-5 NIV

"And God said, 'Let there be a vault between the waters to separate water from water.' So God made the vault and separated the water under the vault from the water above it. And it was so. God called the vault 'sky.' And there was evening, and there was morning—the second day."
Genesis 1:6-8 NIV

"And God said, 'Let the water under the sky be gathered to one place, and let dry ground appear.' And it was so. God called the dry ground 'land,' and the gathered waters he called 'seas.' And God saw that it was good. **Then God said,** 'Let the land produce vegetation: seed-bearing plants and trees on the land that bear fruit with seed in it, according to their various kinds.' And it was so. The land produced vegetation: plants bearing seed according to their kinds and trees bearing fruit with seed in it according to their kinds. And God saw that it was good. And there was evening, and there was morning—the third day."
Genesis 1:9-13 NIV

"And God said, 'Let there be lights in the vault of the sky to separate the day from the night, and let them serve as signs to mark sacred times, and days and years, and let them be lights in the vault of the sky to give light on the earth.' And it was so. God made two great lights—the greater light to govern the day and the lesser light to govern the night. He also made the stars. God set them in the vault of the sky to give light on the earth, to govern the day and the night, and to separate light from darkness. And God saw that it was good. And there was evening, and there was morning
—the fourth day."
Genesis 1:14-19 NIV

And God said, 'Let the water teem with living creatures, and let birds fly above the earth across the vault of the sky.' So God created the great creatures of the sea and every living thing with which the water teems and that moves about in it, according to their kinds, and every winged bird according to its kind. And God saw that it was good. God blessed them and said, 'Be fruitful and increase in number and fill the water in the seas, and let the birds increase on the earth.' And there was evening, and there was morning —the fifth day."

Genesis 1:20-23 NIV

"And God said, 'Let the land produce living creatures according to their kinds: the livestock, the creatures that move along the ground, and the wild animals, each according to its kind.' And it was so. God made the wild animals according to their kinds, the livestock according to their kinds, and all the creatures that move along the ground according to their kinds. And God saw that it was good. **Then God said,** 'Let us make mankind in our image, in our likeness, so that they may rule over the fish in the sea and the birds in the sky, over the livestock and all the wild animals, and over all the creatures that move along the ground.'

So God created mankind in his own image in the image of God he created them; male and female he created them. God blessed them and said to them, 'Be fruitful and increase in number; fill the earth and subdue it. Rule over the fish in the sea and the birds in the sky and over every living creature that moves on the ground.'

Then God said, 'I give you every seed-bearing plant on the face of the whole earth and every tree that has fruit with seed in it. They will be yours for food. And to all the beasts of the earth and all the birds in the sky and all the creatures that move along the ground—everything that has the breath of life in it— I give every green plant for food.' And it was so. God saw all that he had made, and it was very good. And there was evening, and there was morning—the sixth day."

Genesis 1:24-31 NIV

"Thus the heavens and the earth were completed in all their vast array. By the seventh day God had finished the work he had been doing; so on the seventh day he rested from all his work. Then God blessed the seventh day and made it holy, because on it he rested from all the work of creating that he had done."

Genesis 2:1-3 NIV

Glossary

Abound. Flourish; thrive.
… animals abound, a picturesque scene.

Adorned. Decorated; enhanced.
… adorned with hues of endless supply.

Array. Design; display.
… beauty beyond our understanding in a vivid array.

Brilliant. Bright; radiant; vivid.
… and brilliant colors oh so fair …

Burst. Erupted; exploded; surged.
The canvas once blank, burst forth at His voice …

Canvas. Cloth; tarp.
The canvas once blank, burst forth at His voice …

Centuries. Hundreds of years.
… whispering tales of centuries past.

Creative. Gifted; ingenious; original.
Be amazed at God's creative power.

Display. Exhibit; showcase.
Everywhere you look, God's artwork is on display …

Elegant. Beautiful; grand; refined.
With elegant strokes splashed here and there …

Fair. Attractive; lovely.
… and brilliant colors oh so fair …

Feast. Festival; gala; treat.
Gaze upon it all, a feast for the eye.

Flair. Glamor; style.
… set the background with elegance and flair …

Gaze. Admire; gawk; stare.
Gaze upon it all, a feast for the eye.

Gorgeous. Attractive; dazzling; exquisite.
… a gorgeous picture that none can compare.

Grace. Adorn; decorate; enhance.
… adding trees and plants the hillside to grace.

Great I Am. God; Creator.
Only the Great I Am could create so majestic a view.

Hallelujah. Praise; shout for joy or gratitude.
… singing a hallelujah, a heavenly rejoice.

Hues. Tints; tones.
… adorned with hues of endless supply.

Jubilee. Celebration; treat.
… no two paintings can ever be an exact colorful jubilee

Majestic. Awesome; impressive; marvelous.
Only the Great I Am could create so majestic a view.

Masterfully. Excellently; magnificently.
… God's paintings done masterfully?

Mere. Common; plain; simple.
The various colors are beyond what mere man could do

Myriad. Countless; endless.
… a myriad of colors each set in place.

Palette. Set or variety of colors.
His palette fills the land, sea, and sky …

Peaks. Crests; mounts; pinnacles.
The distant peaks of mountain tops …

Glossary

Picturesque. Beautiful; colorful; pleasant.
... animals abound, a <u>picturesque</u> scene.

Radiant. Brilliant; gleaming; glowing.
... the stars, moon, or sun's <u>radiant</u>, pure light ...

Rejoice. Delight; triumph.
... singing a hallelujah, a heavenly <u>rejoice</u>.

Scene. Display; setting; view.
... animals abound, a picturesque <u>scene</u>.

Scurry. Dart; dash; scamper.
Creatures on land that <u>scurry</u> and race ...

Slopes. Descents; hills; tilts.
The distant peaks of mountain tops and <u>slopes</u> as a valley drops ...

Species. Breed; group; kind.
God put each <u>species</u> right into place.

Strokes. Brushes; marks as with a paint brush.
With elegant <u>strokes</u> splashed here and there ...

Various. Assorted; diverse; numerous.
The <u>various</u> colors are beyond what mere man could do.

Vast. Big; endless; huge.
... draw you into a landscape so <u>vast</u> ...

Vibrant. Colorful; dynamic.
Focus in as <u>vibrant</u> blooms dot the space ...

Vivid. Bright; brilliant; striking.
... beauty beyond our understanding in a <u>vivid</u> array.